So You Got a Property, Now What??

To my **dear parents**, whose wisdom and unwavering support have been the cornerstone of my real estate journey.

Mom: The Short-Term Rental Maven

Mom, you are my beacon of insight when it comes to short-term renting. Your knack for turning a humble space into a cozy retreat has inspired me. Late nights discussing Airbnb strategies, pricing models, and guest experiences—those memories are etched in my heart. You taught me that hospitality isn't just about bedsheets and check-ins; it's about creating memorable moments for travelers. Thank you for sharing your expertise and nurturing my passion.

Dad: The Long-Term Rental Guru

Dad, your lessons on long-term renting have shaped my understanding of real estate as an investment. From tenant screening to lease agreements, you've guided me through the intricacies. Your stories of managing properties, dealing with repairs, and handling tenant disputes have been my crash course

in resilience. You taught me that real estate isn't just about bricks and mortar; it's about building relationships and fostering stability. Your patience and practical wisdom have been my compass.
Together, you both helped me overcome hurdles and barriers—whether it was negotiating that first deal or weathering market fluctuations. Your experiences became my roadmap, and your unwavering belief in my potential fueled my determination.
This book stands as a tribute to your love, sacrifice, and shared dreams. May its pages echo the laughter, the late-night discussions, and the triumphs we've celebrated together.
With boundless gratitude,
Clavacia Love

So You Got a Property, Now What??

Maximizing your capabilities with your assets

Author: Clavacia Love

Love Estates Property Management LLC.

CONTENTS

CONTENTS

Introduction

Hey there!

You know, I've been thinking a lot lately about all the ways you can turn a house into a real money-making machine. Seriously, it's like tapping into a goldmine right under your own roof! Picture this: you've got this property, right? And instead of just letting it sit there, collecting dust, why not put it to work for you? That's what I've been diving into lately, and let me tell you, the possibilities are endless.

Imagine transforming that spare room into a cozy guest suite for travelers passing through town. Or converting that empty basement into a trendy Airbnb hotspot, drawing in folks from all corners of the globe. But it doesn't stop there! You can get even more creative by leasing out part of your backyard for events or turning that garage into a workshop space for local artisans. The options are as vast as your imagination!

I've been digging deep into the world of real estate entrepreneurship, and let me tell you, it's like opening up a whole new world of opportunity. From long-term rentals to short-term stays, there's a rental strategy out there for every type of property and every type of owner. And the best part?

You don't need a fancy degree or a million bucks to get started. All you need is a little creativity, some elbow grease, and a willingness to dive in headfirst.

So, buckle up, my friend, because we're about to embark on an exciting journey into the world of property investment and rental entrepreneurship. Get ready to learn, explore, and discover the countless ways you can turn your humble abode into a lucrative income stream. Trust me, once you start thinking outside the box, the sky's the limit!

Let's do this!

Importance of Rental Strategies

Rental strategies play a pivotal role in the success and profitability of real estate ventures, whether for individual property owners, real estate investors, or property management firms. Effective rental strategies encompass a wide range of considerations, including property selection, pricing, marketing, tenant screening, lease negotiation, and ongoing property management.

For property owners and investors, rental strategies directly impact the financial performance and viability of real estate assets. By implementing sound rental strategies, property owners can optimize occupancy rates, maximize rental income, mitigate risks, and enhance the long-term value of their investments. Moreover, strategic rental decisions enable property owners to adapt to changing market conditions, capitalize on emerging trends, and remain competitive in dynamic real estate markets.

Similarly, for tenants and renters, rental strategies are instrumental in securing desirable living or working spaces that align with their needs, preferences, and budgetary constraints. By exploring different rental options, negotiating favorable lease terms, and understanding their rights and obligations as tenants, individuals and businesses can make informed decisions and establish fulfilling living or working environments. For investors this is when utilizing a property management firm can be advantageous given that this is an expert that should be more familiar with the supply and demand of the local area.

In summary, rental strategies serve as the cornerstone of successful real estate transactions, fostering mutually beneficial relationships between landlords and tenants, driving economic growth, and contributing to vibrant and sustainable communities. Understanding the importance of rental strategies empowers stakeholders to navigate the complexities of the rental market, seize opportunities, and achieve their respective goals in the dynamic world of real estate. The purpose of this book is to inform an overview of how this industry works as well as offer a bonus on various ways an individual or group can rent their properties or home!

Definition of Real Estate Rental

The concept of real estate rental encompasses the leasing or renting of property by an individual, group, or organization for residential, commercial, or industrial purposes. It involves the transfer of the right to use and occupy a property in exchange for periodic payments known as "rent". Real estate rental arrangements vary widely in duration, terms, and conditions, ranging from short-term vacation rentals to long-term residential leases and commercial leases spanning several years. This means that there are options of how you are renting and it includes, but is not limited to simply having a traditional family stay in a home year-to-year.

In the realm of real estate, rental agreements typically outline the rights and responsibilities of both landlords and tenants, including matters related to property maintenance, payment schedules, and lease terms. Real estate rental transactions are governed by legal frameworks and regulations established at federal, state, and local levels, ensuring fairness, transparency, and accountability in rental transactions. A simple way of looking at the rental agreement or lease, is a law binding contract.

Understanding the dynamics of real estate rental is essential for property owners, tenants, investors, and professionals in the real estate industry. It involves a multifaceted approach that considers market trends, economic conditions, demographic shifts, and legal considerations. By grasping the intricacies of real estate rental, individuals and organizations can navigate the rental landscape effectively, maximize investment opportunities, and foster mutually beneficial relationships between landlords and tenants. With all of these variables in mind, different rental strategies can tend to be more successful in different areas and locations based off a number of factors. Fortunately, there are no limitations saying that an entrepreneur is unable to make an attempt at various strategies at a single location or property.

Traditional Rental Strategies

In the realm of real estate, traditional rental strategies, particularly long-term residential rentals, form the backbone of the rental market, providing stability, security, and enduring value for landlords and tenants alike. This chapter explores the definition, characteristics, pros and cons, and best practices associated with traditional long-term rental arrangements.

Definition and Characteristics:

Long-term residential rentals encompass rental agreements with extended lease durations, typically ranging from six months to several years. These leases offer tenants the opportunity to establish a stable living arrangement and build roots within a community. Key characteristics of long-term rentals include:

- **Duration:** Long-term leases typically span one year or more, providing tenants with security of tenure and stability.

- **Rental Rates:** Rental rates in long-term leases are often lower compared to short-term rentals, reflecting the extended commitment and reduced turnover costs for landlords.
- **Lease Terms and Conditions:** Long-term leases outline terms and conditions governing the rental agreement, including rent escalation clauses, maintenance responsibilities, and provisions for lease renewal or termination. Long-term rentals differ from short-term vacation rentals in their emphasis on sustained occupancy, community integration, and long-term commitment to the property.

Pros and Cons:

For landlords, long-term residential rentals offer several advantages, including:

- **Stable Income:** Long-term leases provide landlords with predictable rental income and reduced vacancy risks compared to short-term rentals.
- Reduced Turnover: Longer lease durations minimize turnover costs associated with tenant vacancies, leasing commissions, and property marketing expenses.
- **Potential Property Appreciation:** Long-term rentals contribute to property appreciation over time, offering landlords the opportunity to build equity and realize

long-term investment returns. For tenants, long-term rentals provide:

- **Security of Tenure:** Long-term leases afford tenants security and stability in their living arrangements, fostering a sense of belonging and community.
- **Stability:** Long-term rentals offer tenants peace of mind and stability, enabling them to establish roots, maintain social connections, and pursue long-term goals. Despite these benefits, long-term rentals present challenges for both landlords and tenants. Landlords may encounter limited flexibility in adjusting rental rates or modifying lease terms, while tenants may experience restrictions on mobility and flexibility in housing choices.

Best Practices for Landlords and Tenants:

For landlords, best practices in long-term residential rentals include:

- **Property Maintenance:** Landlords should maintain rental properties in good condition, promptly addressing maintenance issues and ensuring compliance with health and safety regulations.
- **Rent Collection:** Establish clear rent payment policies and procedures, including acceptable payment methods, due dates, and consequences for late payments.

- **Tenant Screening:** Conduct thorough tenant screenings, including background checks, credit evaluations, and rental history verifications, to identify reliable and responsible tenants.

- **Legal Compliance:** Familiarize yourself with landlord-tenant laws, fair housing regulations, and local ordinances governing rental properties to ensure legal compliance and mitigate liability risks. For tenants, best practices in long-term rentals involve:

- **Timely Rent Payments:** Honor lease agreements by making timely rent payments each month, avoiding late fees and potential eviction proceedings.

- **Property Upkeep:** Maintain rental properties in good condition, promptly reporting maintenance issues and seeking landlord approval for any alterations or improvements.

- **Adherence to Lease Terms:** Familiarize yourself with lease terms and conditions, including rules regarding pet policies, noise restrictions, and property use, and adhere to these provisions throughout the tenancy.

- **Effective Communication:** Foster open and transparent communication with your landlord, addressing concerns or disputes promptly and seeking mutually beneficial resolutions through constructive dialogue. In summary, traditional long-term residential rentals offer a foundation of stability, security, and value for both landlords and tenants in the dynamic rental market. By understanding the defining characteristics, weighing the pros and cons, and implementing best practices in property management and tenant relations, stakeholders can cultivate mutually beneficial rental relationships and promote long-term success in the rental industry.

Commercial Leasing

Commercial leasing encompasses a diverse array of properties and transactions that facilitate business operations, retail activities, and industrial activities. In this chapter, we explore the different types of commercial properties, leasing terms and negotiation strategies, as well as legal considerations and regulations inherent in commercial leasing agreements.

Types of Commercial Properties:

Commercial properties encompass a wide range of asset classes, each serving distinct business needs and operational requirements:

1. **Office Buildings:** Office buildings are purpose-built structures designed to accommodate professional services, corporate headquarters, and administrative functions. They vary in size, layout, and amenities, ranging from high-rise towers in urban centers to suburban office parks.

2. **Retail Spaces:** Retail spaces include storefronts, shopping centers, and malls that house retail businesses, restaurants, and service providers. These properties typically feature high visibility, foot traffic, and access to transportation hubs.

3. **Industrial Warehouses:** Industrial warehouses are facilities designed for manufacturing, storage, and distribution activities. They range from small-scale warehouses to large logistics centers and fulfillment warehouses, catering to diverse industrial sectors.

4. **Mixed-Use Developments:** Mixed-use developments integrate commercial, residential, and recreational components within a single property, creating vibrant live-work-play environments. These developments offer convenience, diversity, and synergies between different land uses.

Each type of commercial property presents unique characteristics and considerations for landlords and tenants. Office buildings require amenities such as parking facilities, security systems, and access to transportation networks. Retail spaces demand high visibility, foot traffic, and proximity to consumer markets. Industrial warehouses prioritize logistical efficiency, accessibility, and storage capacity. Mixed-use developments seek to balance residential, commercial, and recreational amenities to create cohesive urban environments.

Leasing Terms and Negotiation Strategies:

Commercial leases encompass a range of terms and conditions that govern the landlord-tenant relationship:

1. **Rent Structure:** Commercial leases may feature different rent structures, including triple net leases, gross leases, or modified gross leases, each allocating responsibility for operating expenses, utilities, and maintenance costs differently between landlords and tenants.

2. **Lease Duration and Renewal Options:** Lease durations for commercial properties vary depending on market conditions, tenant preferences, and property characteristics. Landlords and tenants negotiate renewal options, lease terms, and escalation clauses to ensure flexibility and predictability in lease agreements.

3. **Operating Expenses:** Commercial leases outline the allocation of operating expenses, including property taxes, insurance premiums, and maintenance costs. Landlords and tenants negotiate expense caps, pass-through provisions, and auditing rights to manage cost-sharing arrangements effectively.

Negotiation strategies for commercial leases involve understanding market dynamics, assessing property value, and leveraging strengths to secure favorable terms. Landlords seek to maximize rental income, minimize vacancies, and mitigate risk exposure through lease structuring and tenant selection. Tenants aim to minimize occupancy costs, optimize space utilization, and negotiate concessions such as tenant improvement allowances or rent abatements.

Legal Considerations and Regulations:

Commercial leasing agreements are governed by legal frameworks and regulatory requirements that define rights, obligations, and remedies for landlords and tenants:

1. **Common Clauses and Provisions:** Commercial leases include common clauses and provisions addressing rent escalation, lease termination, subletting, default remedies, and dispute resolution mechanisms. These clauses define the rights and responsibilities of both parties and clarify expectations for performance and compliance.

2. **Regulatory Compliance:** Commercial leases must comply with federal, state, and local regulations governing landlord-tenant relationships, fair housing practices, building codes, zoning ordinances, and environmental regulations. Landlords and tenants must understand and adhere to legal requirements to avoid liability risks and ensure contractual enforceability.

3. **Tenant Rights and Dispute Resolution:** Commercial leases protect tenant rights, including the right to quiet

enjoyment, habitable premises, and fair treatment under the law. Dispute resolution mechanisms, such as arbitration, mediation, or litigation, provide avenues for resolving disagreements and enforcing contractual obligations.

In conclusion, commercial leasing entails navigating diverse property types, negotiating complex lease terms, and adhering to legal and regulatory requirements. By understanding the unique characteristics of commercial properties, employing effective negotiation strategies, and ensuring legal compliance, landlords and tenants can forge mutually beneficial leasing agreements that promote business success and mitigate risks in the dynamic commercial real estate market.

Alternative Rental Strategies

In the realm of real estate, alternative rental strategies offer innovative approaches to traditional leasing arrangements, providing flexibility and unique benefits for both landlords and tenants. Two notable alternative rental strategies include Rent-to-Own Agreements and Co-Living Spaces.

Rent-to-Own Agreements

Rent-to-Own agreements, also known as lease-to-own or lease-option agreements, offer tenants the opportunity to lease a property with the option to purchase it at a later date. This arrangement allows tenants to rent the property for a specified period, with a portion of their monthly rent payments allocated towards a future down payment on the property.

1. **Definition and Purpose:**
   - Rent-to-Own agreements enable tenants to gradually transition from renting to homeownership.

- The purpose of these agreements is to provide tenants with time to improve their credit scores, save for a down payment, or resolve other financial issues before committing to a mortgage.

2. **Legal Framework and Contractual Considerations:**
   - Rent-to-Own agreements require clear and comprehensive contracts outlining terms such as lease duration, purchase price, and option fees.
   - Legal considerations include provisions for tenant defaults, property maintenance responsibilities, and dispute resolution mechanisms.

3. **Pros and Cons for Buyers and Sellers:**
   - Opportunity to lock in a purchase price, even if property values increase during the lease period.
   - Time to improve creditworthiness and save for a down payment.
   - Risk of losing option fees and accumulated rent credits if unable to secure financing or complete the purchase.
   - Limited control over property maintenance and appreciation.
   - Potential for higher rent payments and upfront option fees.
   - Reduced vacancy risk and consistent cash flow during the lease period.
   - Risk of property depreciation or market downturns affecting the agreed-upon purchase price.
   - Legal complexities and potential disputes arising from tenant defaults or contract disputes.

Technological Innovations in Real Estate Rentals

As the real estate industry continues to evolve, technological innovations play an increasingly pivotal role in streamlining rental management processes, enhancing tenant experiences, and optimizing property performance. This chapter delves into two key technological innovations in real estate rentals: Rental Management Software and Smart Home Technology.

Rental Management Software:

1. **Features and Benefits:** Rental Management Software (RMS) is a comprehensive solution designed to automate and streamline various aspects of rental property management, including tenant screening, lease administration, rent collection, maintenance tracking, and financial reporting. Key features of RMS include online rent payments, automated lease renewals, maintenance request portals, document management, and tenant communication tools. By centralizing data and automating routine tasks, RMS enables landlords and property managers to improve

operational efficiency, reduce administrative burdens, and enhance tenant satisfaction. The benefits of RMS extend beyond operational efficiencies to include enhanced transparency, accuracy, and scalability in managing rental portfolios. Real-time access to property performance metrics, financial reports, and tenant communications empowers stakeholders to make data-driven decisions and optimize rental strategies for maximum returns.

2. **Popular Platforms and Tools:** The market for Rental Management Software is diverse, with a plethora of platforms and tools catering to the needs of landlords, property managers, and real estate investors. Popular RMS platforms include Buildium, AppFolio, Propertyware, Rent Manager, and Yardi Systems, each offering a unique suite of features and customization options tailored to specific market segments and property types. Additionally, emerging PropTech startups continue to disrupt the industry with innovative solutions addressing niche needs such as vacation rentals, student housing, and multifamily properties. These platforms leverage cloud-based technology, artificial intelligence, and machine learning algorithms to deliver advanced analytics, predictive insights, and personalized user experiences.

3. **Integration with Online Listing Platforms:** RMS platforms often integrate seamlessly with online listing platforms such as Zillow, Trulia, Apartments.com, and Craigslist to streamline the rental listing process and maximize property exposure to prospective tenants. Integration features include automatic listing updates, lead

management, and syndication across multiple channels. By harnessing the power of online listing platforms, landlords and property managers can reach a wider audience, attract qualified leads, and expedite the rental application process. Real-time analytics and performance tracking enable continuous optimization of listing strategies and rental marketing efforts to drive occupancy rates and minimize vacancies.

Smart Home Technology:

1. **Impact on Rental Property Management:** Smart Home Technology encompasses a range of Internet-connected devices and sensors designed to automate and optimize residential environments, enhance security, and improve energy efficiency. In rental properties, smart home devices such as smart thermostats, door locks, security cameras, and lighting systems offer numerous benefits for landlords, tenants, and property managers. By integrating smart home technology into rental properties, landlords can remotely monitor property conditions, control access, and automate routine tasks such as temperature regulation and energy consumption. Real-time alerts and notifications enable proactive maintenance and security

measures, reducing operational costs and minimizing risks of property damage or unauthorized access.

2. **Security and Energy Efficiency Solutions:** Smart home security systems provide tenants with peace of mind by offering customizable security settings, remote monitoring, and surveillance capabilities. Features such as motion sensors, doorbell cameras, and alarm systems deter intruders and enhance overall property security. Additionally, energy-efficient smart devices such as programmable thermostats and smart lighting solutions help tenants reduce utility costs and minimize environmental impact.

3. **Tenant Adoption and Privacy Concerns:** Tenant adoption of smart home technology varies depending on factors such as demographic preferences, technological literacy, and privacy concerns. While many tenants appreciate the convenience and security benefits of smart home devices, others may express reservations regarding data privacy, surveillance, and potential vulnerabilities to hacking or cyber threats. Landlords and property managers must address tenant privacy concerns by implementing robust data security measures, providing clear communication regarding data collection and usage policies, and offering opt-in/opt-out options for smart home features. Transparency and consent are essential in fostering trust and ensuring compliance with data protection regulations such as GDPR and CCPA.

In conclusion, Rental Management Software and Smart Home Technology represent transformative innovations shaping the future of real estate rentals. By leveraging the capabilities of these technologies, landlords, property managers, and tenants can optimize rental operations, enhance living experiences, and unlock new opportunities for sustainable growth and innovation in the dynamic real estate landscape.

Niche Rental Markets: Event Spaces and Venue Rentals

In the diverse landscape of real estate rental, niche markets such as event spaces and venue rentals offer unique opportunities for property owners and entrepreneurs to capitalize on specialized needs and preferences. This chapter explores the dynamics of event spaces and venue rentals, including considerations for identifying profitable locations, managing event planning logistics, and navigating licensing and insurance requirements.

Event Spaces and Venue Rentals:

1. **Identifying Profitable Locations:** Event spaces thrive in locations with high demand for hosting various events, such as weddings, corporate gatherings, and cultural celebrations. Urban centers, tourist destinations, and scenic locales often present lucrative opportunities for venue rentals. Market research and demographic analysis can help identify target audiences and understand their preferences for event venues. Factors such as accessibility,

parking facilities, and proximity to amenities also influence the attractiveness of a location for event rentals.

2. **Event Planning and Logistics:** Successful event spaces prioritize seamless event planning and logistics to enhance the client experience and differentiate themselves in the market. This involves collaborating with event planners, caterers, decorators, and other vendors to coordinate all aspects of event execution. Property owners may invest in versatile spaces that can accommodate a variety of events and offer customizable features such as sound systems, lighting options, and flexible seating arrangements. Effective communication and meticulous attention to detail are paramount in ensuring client satisfaction and fostering long-term relationships.

3. **Licensing and Insurance Requirements:** Venue rentals entail legal and regulatory considerations related to licensing, permits, and insurance coverage. Property owners must obtain appropriate permits for hosting events, adhere to zoning regulations, and ensure compliance with health and safety standards. Insurance coverage is essential to protect against liabilities arising from property damage, personal injury, or unforeseen incidents during events. Comprehensive insurance policies tailored to event spaces provide peace of mind for property owners and mitigate financial risks associated with potential liabilities.

Short-Term Rental Arbitrage:

1. **Definition and Business Model:** Short-term rental arbitrage involves leasing properties from landlords and subletting them on short-term rental platforms such as Airbnb, VRBO, and Booking.com. This business model leverages the difference between long-term lease rates and short-term rental income to generate profit. Arbitrage operators identify properties in desirable locations with high demand for short-term accommodations and negotiate favorable lease terms with landlords. They then furnish and market the properties on rental platforms, managing bookings, guest communication, and property maintenance to maximize occupancy and revenue.

2. **Risks and Rewards:** Short-term rental arbitrage offers the potential for significant returns on investment, particularly in tourist destinations, urban centers, and event-driven markets. The ability to generate cash flow from underutilized properties without long-term commitments appeals to investors and entrepreneurs seeking alternative income streams. However, short-term rental arbitrage is not without risks. Operators face challenges such as fluctuating occupancy rates, seasonal demand variations, regulatory restrictions, and operational expenses. Additionally, dependence on third-party platforms exposes operators to changes in terms of service, algorithm updates, and competition from other hosts.

3. **Compliance with Local Regulations:** Regulatory compliance is a critical aspect of short-term rental arbitrage, as

local jurisdictions increasingly impose restrictions and regulations on short-term rental operations. Operators must familiarize themselves with zoning ordinances, licensing requirements, occupancy limits, and tax obligations applicable to short-term rentals in their target markets. Proactive engagement with regulatory authorities, participation in community forums, and adherence to industry best practices help mitigate compliance risks and build credibility as responsible hosts. Developing contingency plans and diversifying revenue streams can buffer against regulatory changes and market uncertainties in the dynamic landscape of short-term rentals.

In conclusion, niche rental markets such as event spaces and short-term rental arbitrage offer innovative avenues for property owners and entrepreneurs to monetize their assets and meet evolving consumer demands. By understanding the intricacies of these niche markets and implementing strategic approaches to location selection, operational management, and regulatory compliance, stakeholders can unlock the full potential of niche rental opportunities and thrive in the competitive real estate landscape.

Legal and Ethical Considerations in Real Estate Rentals

In the intricate world of real estate rentals, navigating legal and ethical considerations is essential for fostering harmonious landlord-tenant relationships, ensuring compliance with regulatory frameworks, and upholding ethical standards of conduct. This chapter explores key legal and ethical considerations, including landlord-tenant laws and regulations, fair housing practices, and ethical responsibilities of landlords and property managers.

Landlord-Tenant Laws and Regulations:

1. **Federal vs. State Regulations:** Landlord-tenant laws and regulations govern the rights and obligations of landlords and tenants in rental agreements. While federal laws provide overarching guidelines, state laws often vary in scope and detail, addressing issues such as lease agreements, rent

control, security deposits, eviction procedures, and habitability standards. Understanding the interplay between federal and state regulations is crucial for landlords and tenants to ensure compliance and resolve disputes effectively. Legal counsel and resources provided by state housing authorities or landlord-tenant associations can offer valuable insights into specific legal requirements applicable to rental properties.

2. **Eviction Procedures and Tenant Rights:** Eviction procedures and tenant rights are governed by statutory regulations designed to protect tenants from unlawful evictions and provide recourse in case of disputes. Landlords must follow due process and adhere to eviction laws, which typically require providing written notices, obtaining court orders, and adhering to specific timelines for eviction proceedings. Tenants have rights to due process, adequate notice, and opportunities to remedy lease violations before facing eviction. Legal aid organizations and tenant advocacy groups offer resources and assistance to tenants facing eviction, empowering them to assert their rights and seek legal remedies when necessary.

3. **Fair Housing Practices:** Fair housing practices prohibit discrimination on the basis of race, color, national origin, religion, sex, familial status, or disability in housing-related transactions, including rental advertisements, tenant screening, lease negotiations, and property management practices. The Fair Housing Act and subsequent amendments mandate equal treatment and access to housing opportunities for all individuals. Landlords and property

managers must adhere to fair housing laws and implement nondiscriminatory policies and practices in all aspects of rental operations. Training programs, diversity initiatives, and periodic audits can help ensure compliance with fair housing requirements and foster inclusive rental environments.

Ethical Responsibilities of Landlords and Property Managers:

1. **Maintaining Property Standards:** Landlords have ethical responsibilities to maintain safe, habitable, and well-maintained rental properties for tenants. This includes addressing maintenance requests promptly, conducting regular inspections, and addressing health and safety hazards in a timely manner. Property managers play a critical role in upholding property standards by overseeing maintenance activities, coordinating repairs, and ensuring compliance with building codes and regulations. Proactive maintenance and property upkeep enhance tenant satisfaction, minimize liabilities, and preserve property value over time.

2. **Handling Security Deposits and Lease Agreements:** Ethical handling of security deposits and lease agreements is paramount to fostering trust and transparency in landlord-tenant relationships. Landlords must adhere to state

laws governing security deposits, including timely refunding of deposits, itemized deductions for damages, and written notifications of deposit disposition. Lease agreements should clearly outline rights and responsibilities of both parties, including rent payment terms, maintenance obligations, and dispute resolution procedures. Transparent communication and written documentation help mitigate misunderstandings and conflicts throughout the tenancy.

3. **Resolving Disputes and Conflict Resolution Strategies:** Disputes between landlords and tenants are inevitable in rental relationships and may arise from various issues such as rent payments, property maintenance, lease violations, or neighbor disputes. Effective conflict resolution strategies involve open communication, active listening, and collaborative problem-solving. Landlords and property managers should establish clear channels for addressing tenant concerns, providing multiple avenues for feedback and dispute resolution. Mediation, arbitration, or legal remedies may be employed as last resort options for resolving intractable disputes and preserving tenant satisfaction and property integrity.

In conclusion, navigating the legal and ethical landscape of real estate rentals requires diligence, knowledge, and commitment to upholding principles of fairness, integrity, and accountability. By adhering to landlord-tenant laws and regulations, practicing fair housing principles, and embracing ethical responsibilities, landlords and property managers can foster positive rental experiences, build trust with tenants, and contribute to thriving, inclusive communities.

Future Trends and Predictions in Real Estate Rentals

The landscape of real estate rentals is continually evolving in response to shifting demographic trends, technological advancements, and global economic dynamics. This chapter explores key future trends and predictions shaping the future of rental markets, including the impact of demographic shifts, sustainability initiatives, emerging technologies, and challenges and opportunities for real estate investors.

Evolution of Rental Markets:

1. **Impact of Demographic Shifts and Urbanization:** Demographic shifts, including aging populations, urbanization, and changing lifestyle preferences, are driving demand for rental housing in urban centers and metropolitan areas. Millennials and Generation Z cohorts are increasingly prioritizing flexibility, mobility, and access to

urban amenities, fueling demand for rental properties in walkable, transit-oriented neighborhoods. Urbanization trends, coupled with rising housing costs and limited affordability, are reshaping rental markets, leading to densification, mixed-use developments, and innovative housing solutions tailored to urban lifestyles.

2. **Sustainability and Green Building Initiatives:** Sustainability and environmental stewardship are becoming integral considerations in real estate development and rental property management. Green building initiatives, such as energy-efficient design, renewable energy integration, and sustainable materials, are driving demand for eco-friendly rental properties among environmentally-conscious tenants. Sustainability certifications, such as LEED (Leadership in Energy and Environmental Design) and ENERGY STAR, enhance property value, attract tenants, and reduce operating costs over the long term. Real estate investors and developers are increasingly incorporating sustainability principles into their investment strategies to align with market demand and regulatory requirements.

Emerging Technologies and Disruptive Innovations:

1. **Opportunities and Challenges for Real Estate Investors:** Real estate investors are capitalizing on emerging technologies and disruptive innovations to unlock new opportunities and address evolving market dynamics. Proptech (Property Technology) solutions, including AI-powered analytics, virtual reality (VR) tours, blockchain transactions, and predictive maintenance tools, are revolutionizing property management, investment analysis, and tenant engagement. However, rapid technological advancements also present challenges such as cybersecurity risks, data privacy concerns, and regulatory compliance. Real estate investors must embrace innovation while mitigating risks and adapting to changing market conditions to remain competitive and resilient in the digital age.

2. **Globalization and Cross-Border Investments:** Globalization and cross-border investments are reshaping the dynamics of real estate markets, driving capital flows, and diversifying investment portfolios. Real estate investors are increasingly seeking opportunities in international markets, leveraging favorable economic conditions, regulatory environments, and growth potential in emerging economies. Cross-border investments offer investors access to diverse asset classes, geographic diversification, and potential for higher returns. However, geopolitical uncertainties, currency fluctuations, and regulatory complexities pose risks and require careful due diligence and risk management strategies.

3. **Economic and Market Volatility:** Economic and market volatility, including geopolitical tensions, trade

disruptions, and financial instability, pose challenges for real estate investors and rental markets. Economic downturns, recessions, and market corrections can impact property values, rental demand, and investment returns, leading to increased volatility and risk aversion. Adaptive strategies such as portfolio diversification, risk hedging, and liquidity management are essential for navigating uncertain market conditions and mitigating downside risks. Real estate investors must remain vigilant, agile, and resilient in responding to evolving economic and market trends to preserve capital and sustain long-term growth.

In conclusion, the future of real estate rentals is shaped by dynamic trends, technological innovations, and global forces reshaping the way we live, work, and invest. By understanding and anticipating future trends, real estate investors, developers, and property managers can capitalize on emerging opportunities, mitigate risks, and adapt to changing market dynamics to thrive in the evolving landscape of rental markets.

Co-Living Spaces

Co-Living Spaces represent a modern housing concept where residents share living quarters and amenities, fostering a sense of community and collaboration. These spaces offer an alternative to traditional rental arrangements, providing tenants with affordable housing options and opportunities for social interaction.

1. **Concept and Evolution:**
   - Co-Living Spaces originated as a response to urbanization, rising housing costs, and changing lifestyle preferences.
   - The concept emphasizes shared living areas, such as kitchens, living rooms, and common spaces, promoting social engagement and resource sharing among residents.
2. **Community Building and Shared Amenities:**
   - Co-Living Spaces prioritize community-building activities, such as group dinners, workshops, and social events, to foster meaningful connections among residents.
   - Shared amenities may include coworking spaces, fitness centers, laundry facilities, and communal

gardens, enhancing the overall living experience for tenants.

3. **Legal and Operational Challenges:**
    ◦ Legal considerations for co-living operators include zoning regulations, building codes, and tenant rights.
    ◦ Operational challenges may arise from managing shared resources, resolving conflicts among residents, and ensuring compliance with health and safety standards.

In summary, alternative rental strategies like Rent-to-Own Agreements and Co-Living Spaces offer innovative solutions to address evolving housing needs and preferences. By understanding the defining features, legal considerations, and operational challenges associated with these strategies, landlords and tenants can make informed decisions and explore new opportunities in the rental market.

List of rental tools by type

Here's a list of apps or websites for renting residential or commercial spaces, each with a brief description:

Residential Rental Platforms:

Zillow Rentals: Zillow Rentals is a leading online platform for finding apartments, houses, and condos for rent across the United States.

Trulia Rentals: Trulia Rentals offers a user-friendly interface for searching and browsing rental listings, providing detailed information and neighborhood insights.

Apartments.com: Apartments.com is a comprehensive rental website with millions of listings nationwide, featuring apartments, condos, and townhomes for rent.

Rent.com: Rent.com simplifies the rental search process by providing listings, tools, and resources to help renters find their ideal apartment or home.

HotPads: HotPads specializes in apartment and home rentals, offering interactive maps, neighborhood guides, and search filters to help renters find the perfect place.

PadMapper: PadMapper aggregates rental listings from various sources and displays them on a map, allowing users to visualize available properties in their desired location.

Apartment Finder: Apartment Finder provides a comprehensive database of apartments for rent, along with virtual tours, photos, and floor plans to aid in the search process.

Realtor.com Rentals: Realtor.com Rentals offers a wide selection of rental properties, including apartments, houses, and townhomes, with detailed listings and search filters.

Zumper: Zumper is a rental marketplace that connects renters with verified listings, offering a seamless search experience and real-time updates on available properties.

RentCafe: RentCafe provides a convenient platform for renters to search for apartments and rental homes, offering virtual tours, online applications, and rent payment options.

Vacation Rental Platforms:

Airbnb: Airbnb is a global marketplace for short-term vacation rentals, offering a diverse range of accommodations, from private rooms to entire homes.

Vrbo (formerly HomeAway): Vrbo specializes in vacation rentals, featuring beach houses, cabins, and condos for rent in popular destinations worldwide.

FlipKey: FlipKey offers vacation rentals with a focus on traveler reviews and ratings, helping guests find trusted accommodations for their next getaway.

Tripping.com: Tripping.com aggregates vacation rental listings from multiple platforms, allowing users to compare prices and amenities across different properties.

Homestay: Homestay offers unique accommodations with local hosts, providing travelers with authentic experiences and insights into the culture of their destination.

Booking.com: Booking.com features a wide range of accommodations, including hotels, apartments, and vacation homes, with flexible booking options and competitive rates.

Expedia: Expedia offers vacation rentals along with flights, hotels, and activities, providing travelers with comprehensive travel planning and booking services.

Travelocity: Travelocity allows users to book vacation rentals, flights, hotels, and rental cars, offering deals and discounts for travelers on a budget.

Commercial Rental Platforms:

LoopNet: LoopNet is a commercial real estate marketplace that connects tenants, investors, and brokers with office spaces, retail properties, and industrial buildings.

CoStar: CoStar provides comprehensive data and analytics for commercial real estate professionals, including listings, market research, and investment insights.

CommercialCafe: CommercialCafe offers listings for office spaces, coworking spaces, and retail properties, along with tools for leasing and property management.

42Floors: 42Floors is a commercial real estate search engine that helps tenants find office spaces, coworking spaces, and retail locations in their desired area.

OfficeSpace.com: OfficeSpace.com provides listings for office spaces, coworking spaces, and executive suites, helping businesses find the right workspace for their needs.

Peerspace: Peerspace offers unique event spaces and venues for rent, including commercial buildings, studios, and lofts, perfect for meetings, parties, and photo shoots.

Storefront: Storefront connects brands and businesses with short-term retail space rentals for pop-up shops, product launches, and events in prime locations.

Rofo: Rofo helps businesses find office and industrial spaces for rent, offering detailed listings, search filters, and tools for negotiating leases.

LiquidSpace: LiquidSpace is a flexible workspace platform that allows businesses to book office spaces, meeting rooms, and coworking spaces on-demand.

PivotDesk: PivotDesk facilitates office sharing and subleasing arrangements, connecting companies with excess office space to businesses in need of flexible workspace.

Desktime: Desktime provides access to coworking spaces and shared offices worldwide, offering hourly, daily, and monthly rental options for freelancers and remote workers.

ShareDesk: ShareDesk is a global coworking marketplace that connects professionals with coworking spaces, offering a network of flexible workspaces for individuals and teams.

Workthere: Workthere is a platform that helps businesses find flexible office space solutions, including serviced offices, co-working spaces, and virtual offices.

Flexe: Flexe offers on-demand warehousing solutions for businesses in need of temporary or flexible storage space, with a network of warehouse facilities across the U.S.

Breather: Breather provides on-demand meeting rooms, private offices, and workspaces in major cities, offering flexible rental options for professionals and teams.

Splacer: Splacer offers unique event spaces and venues for rent, including lofts, galleries, and warehouses, ideal for corporate events, weddings, and private parties.

Spacebase: Spacebase is a platform that helps users find and book meeting rooms, conference venues, and event spaces worldwide, with easy online booking and payment.

TheSquareFoot: TheSquareFoot provides tools and resources for finding and leasing commercial real estate, including office spaces, retail properties, and industrial buildings.

Convene: Convene offers flexible meeting and event spaces in major cities, providing state-of-the-art facilities and hospitality services for corporate gatherings and conferences.

Showplace: Showplace is a platform for booking event spaces and venues for trade shows, exhibitions, and conferences, offering customizable options and support services.

MeetingPackage: MeetingPackage helps businesses find and book meeting rooms and conference venues worldwide, offering transparent pricing and instant booking confirmation.

Industrious: Industrious provides premium coworking spaces and private offices in prime locations, catering to professionals and companies seeking flexible workspace solutions.

Knotel: Knotel offers flexible office spaces and custom workspace solutions for businesses of all sizes, with tailored design and amenities to meet specific needs.

Serendipity Labs: Serendipity Labs provides upscale coworking spaces and shared offices with hospitality services and flexible membership options for individuals and teams.

Workbar: Workbar offers coworking spaces and shared offices in Massachusetts, providing members with access to a network of workspaces and amenities.

SpacesWorks: SpacesWorks provides coworking spaces and flexible office solutions in vibrant locations worldwide, offering collaborative environments and business services.

WeWork: WeWork offers coworking spaces, private offices, and shared workspaces in major cities, fostering community and collaboration among members.

Regus: Regus provides flexible workspace solutions, including serviced offices, virtual offices, and coworking spaces, with locations worldwide for businesses of all sizes.

LiquidSpace: LiquidSpace is a flexible workspace platform that allows businesses to book office spaces, meeting rooms, and coworking spaces on-demand.

These platforms offer a variety of options for renting residential properties, vacation homes, and commercial spaces, catering to different preferences, needs, and budgets. Here are some of my favorite strategies highlighted on the following pages!

Closing

As we conclude our exploration of the dynamic world of real estate rentals, it is essential to reflect on the key concepts, strategies, and opportunities discussed throughout this book. From understanding the nuances of rental markets to navigating legal and ethical considerations, real estate professionals play a pivotal role in shaping the rental landscape and fostering thriving communities.

Recap of Key Concepts and Strategies:

Throughout this book, we have delved into various aspects of real estate rentals, including market dynamics, rental strategies, technological innovations, and future trends. We have explored traditional and alternative rental models, examined legal and ethical considerations, and discussed emerging opportunities and challenges in the rental industry.

Key concepts highlighted include:

- Understanding rental market dynamics and demographic trends.
- Leveraging technological innovations to streamline rental operations and enhance tenant experiences.
- Navigating legal and ethical considerations, including landlord-tenant laws, fair housing practices, and sustainability initiatives.
- Identifying opportunities for growth and investment in evolving rental markets.
- Implementing strategic approaches to property management, tenant relations, and conflict resolution.

Call to Action for Real Estate Professionals:

As real estate professionals, it is incumbent upon us to leverage our knowledge, expertise, and resources to drive positive change and innovation in the rental industry. We must embrace continuous learning, adapt to evolving market trends, and prioritize ethical standards of conduct in our professional endeavors.

Our call to action includes:

- Committing to excellence in property management, tenant relations, and customer service.

- Advocating for inclusive and sustainable rental practices that promote equity, diversity, and environmental stewardship.
- Engaging with industry peers, stakeholders, and community partners to share best practices, foster collaboration, and promote industry-wide standards of excellence.
- Embracing technological innovations and disruptive trends to enhance operational efficiency, optimize investment strategies, and deliver value to tenants and investors alike.

Resources for Further Learning and Exploration:

As we embark on our journey to advance the field of real estate rentals, it is essential to seek out resources for further learning, exploration, and professional development. A wealth of resources, including industry publications, educational programs, professional associations, and networking opportunities, are available to support our growth and success in the rental industry.

Recommended resources include:

- Industry publications and journals providing insights into market trends, best practices, and emerging innovations.

- Continuing education programs, certifications, and seminars offered by reputable institutions and professional organizations.
- Professional associations and networking events connecting real estate professionals with peers, mentors, and industry experts.
- Online platforms, webinars, and podcasts featuring thought leaders, experts, and practitioners sharing valuable insights and perspectives on rental industry trends and strategies.

In conclusion, the journey of real estate rentals is a dynamic and ever-evolving one, shaped by the collective efforts and contributions of real estate professionals committed to excellence, integrity, and innovation. By embracing the principles of lifelong learning, collaboration, and ethical stewardship, we can chart a course toward a future of sustainable growth, prosperity, and thriving communities in the rental industry.

Top Picks!

Here are some of my favorite apps for renting spaces!

Airbnb

Airbnb is a platform that allows individuals to rent out their properties, whether it's a single bedroom, an entire house, a cozy cabin, or even a luxurious mansion, to travelers looking for accommodations. It's like a marketplace where hosts list their properties, set their own prices, and connect with guests from around the world.

Whether you have a spare room or an entire property, you can list it on Airbnb for short-term stays, ranging from a single night to several months or even years. Guests can search for properties based on their preferences, budget, and desired location, and book directly through the platform.

For hosts, Airbnb offers flexibility and control over their rental arrangements. They can choose the dates when their property is available, set house rules, and communicate with guests to ensure a smooth and enjoyable stay.

Overall, Airbnb provides an opportunity for hosts to earn extra income by renting out their space to travelers, while guests can enjoy unique and personalized accommodations wherever their adventures take them.

VRBO

Imagine having a beautiful vacation home, cozy cabin, or spacious condo that you're not using all the time. Now, imagine being able to rent it out to travelers and make some extra cash. That's where VRBO comes in.

VRBO, which stands for Vacation Rental By Owner, is a platform that allows property owners to list their homes, cabins, condos, and even mansions for short-term rentals. It's like having your own mini-hotel, but without all the hassle.

Here's how it works: You sign up on VRBO, list your property, set your own prices, and voila! Travelers from all over the world can browse your listing, book their stay, and pay you directly through the platform.

The best part? You can manage everything right from your phone. From updating your listing to communicating with guests to handling reservations, it's all super easy and convenient.

Whether you're looking to make some extra money from your vacation home or you're a traveler in search of unique accommodations, VRBO has got you covered. So why let that beautiful property of yours sit empty when you can turn it into a money-making machine?

Neighbor

You know that garage or storage shed you have sitting there, collecting dust and not being used to its full potential? Well, let me tell you about Neighbor. It's this awesome app that lets you turn that unused space into cold, hard cash by renting it out to people in your community who need extra storage.

Here's how it works: You sign up on Neighbor, list your garage or storage shed, set your own price, and boom! People looking for storage space can find your listing, book it, and start storing their stuff right away.

It's like Airbnb, but for storage space! And the best part? You don't have to lift a finger. Neighbor handles all the details, from payments to insurance, so you can sit back, relax, and watch the money roll in.

So why let that valuable space go to waste when you can turn it into a steady stream of income? With Neighbor, it's easy, convenient, and a great way to make some extra cash without any hassle.

Furnished Finder

Ever heard of Furnished Finder? It's this awesome platform that lets you turn your spare space into extra cash by renting it out to travel nurses and other medical professionals who need short-term furnished housing.

Here's the scoop: You know that spare room or furnished apartment you've got just sitting there? Well, with Furnished Finder, you can list it on their platform, set your own rates, and connect with traveling medical professionals looking for a place to stay.

It's like Airbnb, but specifically for healthcare travelers! And get this - these folks are usually in town for weeks or months at a time, so you can count on a steady stream of income without the hassle of constantly finding new guests.

Furnished Finder takes care of all the details, from bookings to payments, so you can sit back and watch the money roll in. Plus, it's a great way to meet new people and help out those who are doing important work in your community.

So why not put that extra space to good use and make some extra cash while you're at it? With Furnished Finder, it's easy, convenient, and a win-win for everyone involved.

Swimply

Swimply is like Airbnb, but for pools! You know that beautiful pool sitting in your backyard, just waiting to be used? Well, with Swimply, you can rent it out to people in your area who are looking for a private pool experience.

Here's how it works: You list your pool on Swimply, set your own rates, and let people know when it's available. Whether it's for a day of relaxation, a pool party, or just some fun in the sun, there are tons of folks out there looking to make a splash.

The best part? You get to make some extra cash without any extra effort. Swimply handles all the details, from bookings to payments, so you can sit back and enjoy the sunshine while your pool pays for itself.

So why let that amazing pool go to waste when you can turn it into a money-making machine? With Swimply, it's easy, convenient, and a great way to make some extra cash off your backyard oasis.

Swimmy

You know that awesome pool or hot tub you just got for your place? Well, get this – there's this app called Swimmy that lets you rent out your pool to people in your area who are looking for a private swimming experience.

It's seriously genius! You list your pool on Swimmy, set your own rates, and let people know when it's available. Whether it's for a relaxing swim, a poolside barbecue, or just soaking up some sun, there are tons of folks out there who would love to use your pool.

And here's the best part – you get to make some extra cash while your pool gets put to good use! Swimmy takes care of all the details, from bookings to payments, so you can just sit back and watch the money roll in.

I mean, how awesome is that? Your pool becomes a money-making machine, and you get to enjoy it whenever you want too. It's like having your own private resort right in your backyard!

So why not give it a try? With Swimmy, it's easy, convenient, and a great way to make some extra cash off your new pool or hot tub.

My Private Pool

AUTHOR: CLAVACIA LOVE

My Private Pool is an innovative app designed to help pool owners monetize their pools by renting them out to individuals seeking private swimming experiences. Through the app, pool owners can list their pools, set availability, and establish rental rates. Users can browse available pools in their area, book time slots, and enjoy exclusive access to the pool during their rental period. This platform offers a convenient way for pool owners to generate extra income while providing renters with a unique and private swimming experience.

Giggster

AUTHOR: CLAVACIA LOVE

Giggster is a versatile platform that connects people in need of unique spaces with property owners willing to rent them out for various purposes. The app offers a wide range of spaces suitable for photo shoots, film productions, events, and more. Users can browse through a diverse selection of locations including trendy lofts, spacious warehouses, picturesque gardens, cozy cabins, and even upscale mansions. Whether you're planning a photo shoot, filming a commercial, hosting a party, or organizing a corporate event, Giggster provides access to an array of creative and distinctive spaces to suit every need and budget.

Rent My Equipment

I just found out about this awesome app called Rent My Equipment, and I had to tell you about it! It's perfect for folks like us who are into DIY projects or have hobbies like photography. Here's the scoop: Rent My Equipment allows you to rent out your extra equipment to people who need it for their own projects.

So, if you've got a bunch of power tools, woodworking gear, or even photography equipment lying around unused, you can list them on the app and make some extra cash. It's a win-win situation – you get to earn money from equipment you already own, and others get access to tools and gear they might not have otherwise.

It's super convenient and a great way to put your equipment to work when you're not using it. Plus, you get to help out fellow DIY enthusiasts and photographers in the process.

Splacer

Have you heard of Splacer? It's an amazing app that lets you discover and book unique spaces for all sorts of events and gatherings. Whether you're planning a corporate meeting, a birthday party, a photo shoot, or even a pop-up shop, Splacer has got you covered.

The best part? Splacer offers a wide variety of spaces to choose from, including lofts, galleries, warehouses, studios, rooftops, and more. These spaces are not your typical venues – they're filled with character and charm, perfect for adding a touch of uniqueness to any event.

With Splacer, you can find the perfect space to suit your needs, whether you're hosting an intimate gathering or a large-scale event. It's easy to use, convenient, and opens up a world of possibilities for creating memorable experiences.

Peerspace

Peerspace is a versatile online marketplace that connects professionals and creators with unique spaces for various creative and productive purposes. Here's a concise overview:

1. **What is Peerspace?**
    - Peerspace is a platform where individuals and businesses can **book and list** distinctive spaces that were previously **underutilized or unavailable to the public.**
    - These spaces range from **lofts and studios** to **mansion-like venues** and **storefronts.**
    - Whether you're planning a corporate meeting, a social event, a photoshoot, or any other creative endeavor, Peerspace helps you find the perfect space to bring your ideas to life.

2. **How Does Peerspace Work?**
    - **Listing Spaces**: If you own a unique space, you can **list it on Peerspace.** Showcase your property's features, amenities, and availability.
    - **Booking Spaces**: As a guest, you can **browse and book spaces** that suit your needs. Whether it's a one-day offsite or a longer-term rental, Peerspace makes it easy.
    - **Earning Income**: Here's where the money comes in! By hosting your space on Peerspace, you can **earn extra income.** List your space for free, set your own rates, and rent it out on dates that work for you.

3. **Why Peerspace Matters?**
    - **Inspiration**: Access to inspiring spaces fuels creativity and innovation for professionals of all kinds.
    - **Community Impact**: Peerspace enables local businesses to **sustain healthy operations** by sharing their spaces with others.
    - **Unlocking Potential**: Previously overlooked spaces now become vibrant hubs for collaboration, events, and artistic expression.

In summary, Peerspace bridges the gap between unique spaces and those seeking them, fostering creativity, community, and financial opportunities.

Sniffspot

Sniffspot is like the **Airbnb for dog parks**. Let me break it down for you:

1. **What Is Sniffspot?**

   - Sniffspot is a **community marketplace** that connects dog owners with property owners who have **unique outdoor spaces.**
   - These spaces can be **backyards, large open fields, or other private areas.**
   - As a dog owner, you can **rent these spaces by the hour** for your furry friend to enjoy some exercise and playtime.

2. **How Does It Work?**

   - **Browse Locations**: Start by browsing the available Sniffspot locations. These are people's backyards or open fields that you can rent.
   - **Reserve Your Spot**: Once you find a location you like, simply **reserve your spot**. Read the location description to understand if it's fully fenced or an open space.
   - **Private Bookings**: All bookings are **private**, meaning that during your reserved time, **no other dogs, domestic animals, or people** will be in the spot besides those you bring with you.
   - **Stay Responsible**: Sniffspot is **not a dog daycare.** As a guest, you remain **responsible for your dog at all times** during your visit.

3. **Why Sniffspot Matters?**

- **Safety**: Safety is a top priority. Sniffspot ensures that the spaces are secure and suitable for dogs.
- **Community Impact**: By renting out your backyard, you contribute to a **community of dog lovers** who need safe places for their pets.
- **Extra Income**: If you have a great backyard, you can **earn extra income** by listing it on Sniffspot.

In summary, Sniffspot provides a win-win situation: dog owners get a safe and private place for their pups, and property owners can turn their unused outdoor spaces into a valuable resource.

Wag

If you're a homeowner who loves dogs, you can **easily earn money** by dog sitting using the mobile app **Wag**. Here's how it works:

1. **What Is Wag?**

   - **Wag** is an app that connects dog owners with **trusted dog sitters**.
   - As a dog sitter on Wag, you'll have the opportunity to care for dogs in your own home or provide dog-walking services.

2. **How to Get Started:**
   - **Sign Up**: Download the **Wag app** and sign up as a dog sitter.
   - **Experience**: You should have some **previous experience** with dogs, as this will be beneficial.
   - **Safety and Care**: Wag will test you on **dog safety and care**, ensuring that you're well-prepared.
   - **Create Your Profile**: Set up your profile, including details about your home, availability, and services you can offer.

3. **Earning Potential:**

   - **Flexible Schedule**: You can create your own schedule and work as much or as little as you want.
   - **Rates**: Set your own **dog-sitting rates**. Wag allows you to choose what you're comfortable with.

- **Base Fee**: Wag has a base fee structure, so there's no need to negotiate with dog owners.
- **Tips**: You can also earn **tips** from satisfied clients.

4. How Much Can You Make?

- On average, Wag dog sitters can make up to **$500 per month** by sitting dogs just **3 times a week**.
- If you have more time to spare, the earning potential is even higher.

In summary, if you're a dog-friendly homeowner, Wag provides a convenient way to turn your love for dogs into extra income while providing a valuable service to pet owners.

AUTHOR: CLAVACIA LOVE

Zillow

As a homeowner, using the **Zillow Rental Manager** app on your phone or laptop to rent out your property is straightforward and efficient. Here's a brief breakdown:

1. **Sign Up or Log In**:

    ◦ Visit the Zillow Rental Manager website or download the **Zillow Rental Manager app**.
    ◦ Create an account if you're new, or log in if you already have one1.

2. **List Your Property**:

    ◦ Click on "List your properties for free."
    ◦ Provide details about your home, including square footage, bedrooms, bathrooms, and any appealing features.
    ◦ Upload high-quality photos to showcase your property.

3. **Set Rent and Lease Terms**:

    ◦ Specify the **monthly rent, security deposit**, and **pet policy**.
    ◦ Define lease terms, such as duration and any additional requirements.

4. **Tenant Screening**:

    ◦ Zillow integrates tenant screening tools.
    ◦ Receive applications, credit reports, background checks, and eviction history all in one place2.

5. **Manage Applications**:

   - Review applicant information and choose the best fit.
   - Communicate with potential tenants through the app.

6. **Sign the Lease**:

   - Create a rental lease using Zillow's online lease builder.
   - Customize it based on local laws or upload your own lease.
   - E-sign the lease with your renters3.

7. **Collect Rent Payments**:

   - Zillow handles rent collection.
   - Rent, utilities, and move-in fees are deposited directly into your bank account at no cost to you4.

8. **Premium Listing (Optional)**:

   - For increased exposure, consider upgrading to a premium listing.
   - Track performance data and trends to price your rental competitively4.

In summary, Zillow Rental Manager streamlines the process, making it easy for homeowners to list, screen tenants, sign leases, and manage payments—all from one convenient platform.

Zillow 3D tour

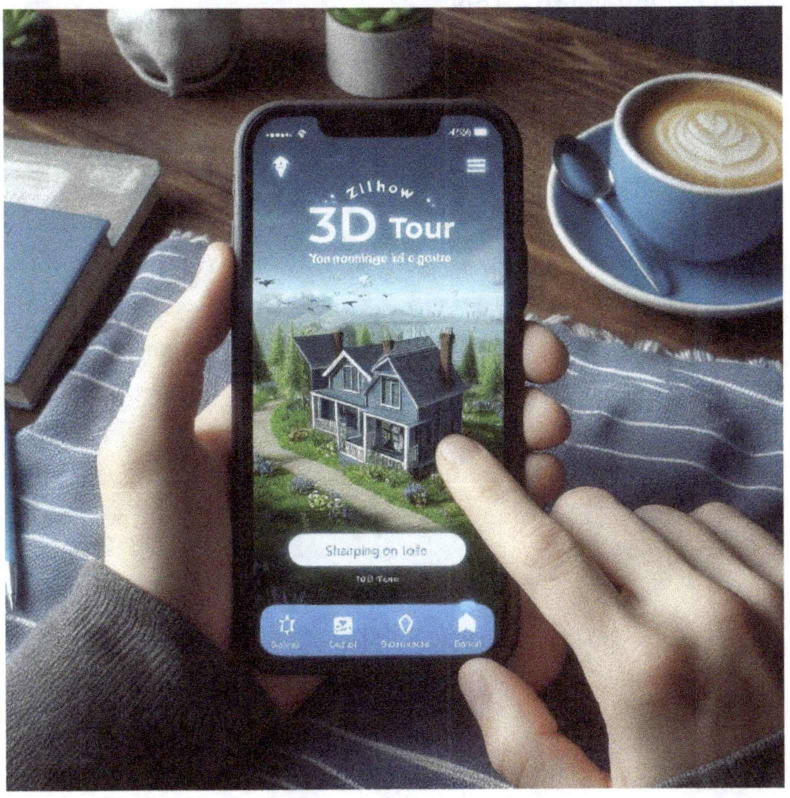

Let's explore how the **Zillow 3D Home app** simplifies creating virtual property tours and enhances your home's visibility:

1. **Download the App:**

   - **Free and User-Friendly**: Start by downloading the **Zillow 3D Home app** on your **iPhone** or **Android** device. It's **totally free** and easy to use.

2. **Capture Every Room:**

   - **Supported Devices**: Use a **supported iPhone, Android smartphone**, or a **360-degree camera** (such as Ricoh Theta or Insta360).
   - **Panoramas**: Capture **panoramas** of each room in your home. The app will automatically create both a **3D Home tour** and an **interactive floor plan**.

3. **Enhance the Experience:**

   - **Immersive Tours**: Listings with 3D Home tours and interactive floor plans are made to be explored.
   - **Layout Understanding**: With every room you capture, potential buyers can **understand the layout** and imagine what it would be like to call your home their own.

4. **Stand Out from the Crowd:**

   - **Boost Visibility**: Listings with 3D Home tours receive **60% more views** than those without.

- **Interactive Floor Plans**: Homes with an **Interactive Floor Plan** are saved **79% more** by interested buyers.
- **Share Everywhere**: Publish your 3D Home tour and floor plan on your listing, social media, MLS, and your website.

5. **Sell Virtually**:

- **Dynamic Floor Plans**: **69%** of home buyers agree that a dynamic floor plan helps them determine if a home is right for them.
- **Seal the Deal**: 3D Home tours and interactive floor plans make listings more interesting and people more interested.

6. **What People Are Saying**:

- Greg Dallaire from Dallaire Realty: "We leverage Zillow 3D Home tours to get more traffic to our properties."
- Becky Garcia from The Garcia Group: "The equipment is super easy to use, the app is user-friendly, and it's offered at no charge."

In summary, the Zillow 3D Home app empowers you to create captivating virtual tours, making your home stand out in a competitive market. Download the app now and showcase your property like never before!

AUTHOR: CLAVACIA LOVE

Affordable housing

As a **private property owner**, utilizing **AffordableHousing.com** to find **Section 8 tenants** and receive **guaranteed rents** from government housing is straightforward and beneficial. Here's a breakdown:

1. **What Is Section 8?**

   - The **Section 8 Housing Choice Voucher Program** is the largest and most successful low-income housing assistance program in the country.
   - Property owners who participate in Section 8 benefit because **up to 100% of the rent is paid by the government.**
   - As long as lease terms and property conditions are maintained, the rent is virtually guaranteed and sent to the owner every month.

2. **How Does Section 8 Work?**

   - Approximately **2.3 million households** receive federal rental assistance via Section 8.
   - **Federally funded** by the U.S. Department of Housing and Urban Development (HUD), Section 8 is administered locally by over **2,400 Public Housing Agencies (PHAs)** across the country.

3. **Getting a Section 8 Voucher:**

   - Obtaining a Section 8 voucher is **not easy** due to funding limitations.

- Many waiting lists for Section 8 assistance are **closed or open sporadically**, making it challenging to get on a waiting list.
- PHAs have different local priorities and methods for selecting applicants, including local residency preferences.

4. **AffordableHousing.com's Role:**

- **Streamlined Process:** AffordableHousing.com partners with many PHAs to simplify finding and qualifying for affordable housing programs like Section 8.
- **Universal Application:** Use the **RevoList universal application** to increase your chances of getting a Section 8 voucher quickly.

5. **Listing Your Property on AffordableHousing.com:**

- **Free Listing**: List your property for free on AffordableHousing.com.
- **Section 8 Renters**: Section 8 renters actively use this platform to find housing.
- **Guaranteed Rent**: By participating, you can receive **guaranteed rent payments** from government housing.

In summary, AffordableHousing.com connects property owners with Section 8 tenants, simplifying the process and ensuring stable income while assisting lower-income families.

Rooms for Rent

AUTHOR: CLAVACIA LOVE

Rooms for rent is a roommate finder app that simplifies the process of finding a compatible roommate to share a home. Whether you're looking for property rentals, apartment shares, or renting spare rooms, this app provides a trusted marketplace. It's a convenient solution for those seeking affordable housing arrangements.

Clavacia Love REI, influencer, and mentor.
Copyright © 2024 by Love Estates Property Management LLC

First Printing, 2024